W9-AMP-842

BUTTERFIELD SCHOOL
1441 LAKE STREET
LIBERTYVILLE IL 60048

Author:
Kathryn Senior is a former biomedical
research scientist who studied at Cambridge
University for an advanced degree in
microbiology. After four years in research, she
joined the world of publishing as an editor of
children's science books. She has now been a
full-time science writer for ten years.

Artist:
David Antram was born in Brighton in 1958.
He studied at Eastbourne College of Art and then
worked in advertising for fifteen years before
becoming a full-time artist. He has illustrated
many children's non-fiction books.

Series Creator:
David Salariya was born in Dundee, Scotland.
He has illustrated a wide range of books and has
created and designed many new series for
publishers both in the U.K. and overseas. In 1989,
he established The Salariya Book Company. He
lives in Brighton with his wife, illustrator
Shirley Willis, and their son Jonathan.

Editor:
Karen Barker Smith

Assistant Editor:
Stephanie Cole

Created, designed, and produced by
The Salariya Book Company Ltd
Book House, 25 Marlborough Place,
Brighton BN1 1UB

Please visit the Salariya Book Company at:
www.salariya.com

ISBN 0-531-14605-7 (Lib. Bdg.)
ISBN 0-531-16366-0 (Pbk.)

Published in the United States by Franklin Watts
A Division of Scholastic Inc.
90 Sherman Turnpike, Danbury, CT 06816

A CIP catalog record for this title is
available from the Library of Congress.

Repro by Modern Age.

Printed and bound in Belgium.

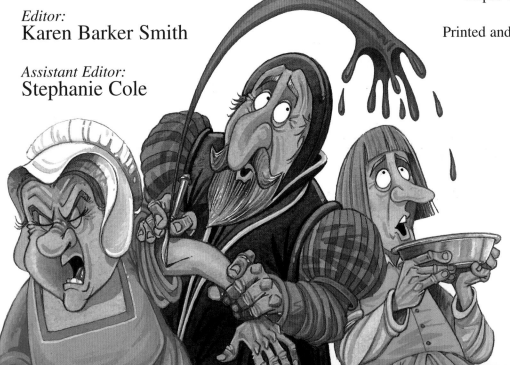

You Wouldn't Want to Be Sick in the 16th Century!

Written by
Kathryn Senior

Illustrated by
David Antram

> You might feel just a little twinge…

Diseases You'd Rather Not Catch

Created and designed by
David Salariya

W
FRANKLIN WATTS
A Division of Scholastic Inc.

NEW YORK • TORONTO • LONDON • AUCKLAND • SYDNEY
MEXICO CITY • NEW DELHI • HONG KONG
DANBURY, CONNECTICUT

Contents

Introduction

Your name is Nicholas Knight, and you are a barber surgeon in the 16th century, known in England as Tudor times. You were born in 1533, the same year as Queen Elizabeth I. Cities and towns in Tudor times are overcrowded and filthy. Animals live in houses, and waste is slopped right onto the street. It is no great surprise that people often get sick. When they do, there are no hospitals or doctors with a choice of medicines. The medicine that is available is weird and sometimes horrifying.

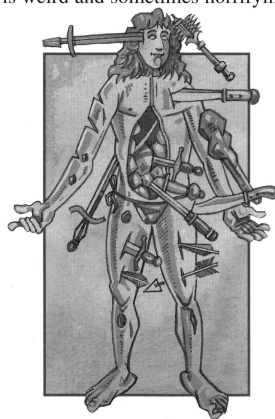

Your father is eager for you to be an important man in society. You showed an early interest in learning, so you have been sent to London at the age of twelve to become a barber surgeon's apprentice. London is an exciting place, but as you begin to learn the craft of medicine, you soon learn why you wouldn't want to be sick in the 16th century!

A Tough Start

Y ou arrive in London to work with your master in 1545, when you are twelve years old. You have to share a room in your master's house with another young apprentice. You spend long days reading your master's books and listening to him talk about his work. After a few weeks, he decides to take you out to see the sick.

One way to diagnose illnesses is to examine patients' urine. Your master uses a collection of glass pots to examine the urine three times: once when it is fresh, again when it has cooled for about an hour, and then when it is completely cold. Sometimes you even have to taste the urine to see if it is sweet or sour!

What You Will Need:

GLASS POTS in which to examine the urine. You hold the pot up to the light to see its color and to see if it contains any particles. You then consult a book (below) to make a diagnosis.

A COLOR WHEEL that you use to compare the color of the urine. The colors are linked to different types of illnesses.

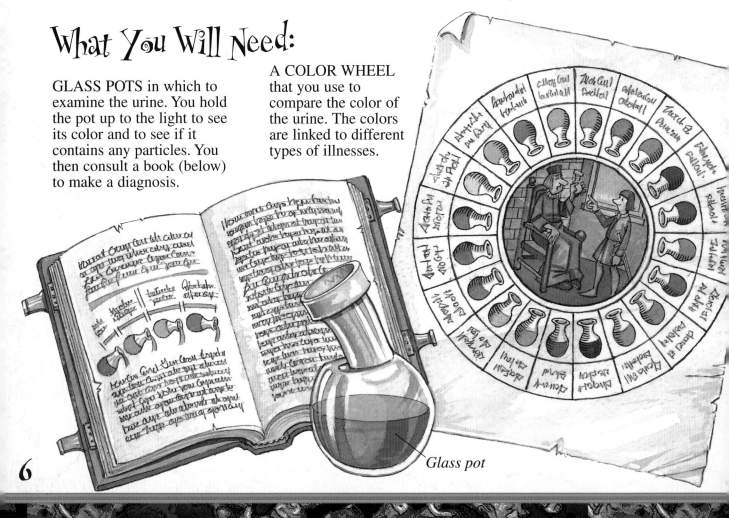

Glass pot

Padua – Center of Learning

BEFORE VESALIUS wrote his great anatomy book, people thought the inside of the body looked like this. No wonder doctors had trouble deciding what was wrong with the sick!

THE MEDICAL SCHOOL in Padua is one of the first to be built in Europe.

In the second year of your training as a barber surgeon, you travel to Padua, Italy. The medical school there is very famous. You see some anatomy lectures given by a young teacher named Andreas Vesalius. He is very popular, and everybody crushes into the dissection hall to watch what he does and listen to what he says.

Seeing a body being cut open and peeled apart piece by piece is both exciting and frightening. You have never seen anything like this in London. Vesalius has been working on his own book about anatomy, and you find a copy of it in the library. The drawings show what is inside the body in great detail. It looks so strange that you can hardly believe all of it is inside you.

Handy Hint

Get an artist with a strong stomach to make sketches of dissections. You don't want your artist to faint or get sick halfway through and only draw part of the body.

VESALIUS starts a strong tradition of anatomy at Padua. Eventually, a circular lecture theater is built (below), specially designed to give everyone a good view.

And if we just peel this back, like so...

Blood, Glorious Blood!

What You Will Need:

A MAP of the veins of the body, showing the best points to get blood.

SEVERAL KNIVES and puncture pins for cutting into different veins. These should all be sharpened regularly.

arber surgeons believe illness is caused by "badness" in the blood, and letting the "badness" out of the body will cure the patient. One of their main treatments is called blood-letting. The barber surgeon uses special tools to cut open a vein and then catches the blood in a shallow bowl. If the patient is not very sick, losing a little blood probably does no harm. The problem is that barber surgeons don't know when to stop. Many patients die from the treatment after losing several pints of blood. A gentler method is to use blood-sucking worms called leeches.

AT AGE FOURTEEN, you have the terrifying experience of going to the Royal Court with your master to treat King Henry VIII. Despite treatments of bleeding, rest, and herbal potions, Henry soon dies. You are sad that the old King is dead but glad that you don't have to go back there again!

Handy Hint

Slither

Make sure that you stop the bleeding and remove all the leeches before you leave. You don't want your patient to bleed to death from your treatment.

When Humor Wasn't Funny

Alternative Cures:

PUTTING A SOOTHING LOTION on the weapon that has wounded a soldier will cure that soldier instantly.

ASTROLOGY is widely used by Tudor doctors. They ask for a patient's birth sign and make a diagnosis according to the position of the stars.

ACCORDING to the Tudors, toads held next to a wart will cure the nasty hard lump of skin very quickly.

In the 16th century, people use the word "humor" to describe the fluids that make up the human body. They believe the theories of a doctor named Galen, who lived in ancient Greece. Galen said that the normal healthy person has four humors in his or her body: blood, phlegm, black bile, and yellow bile. Blood is hot and wet; phlegm is cold and wet; black bile is cold and dry; and yellow bile is hot and dry. According to Galen, when all four humors are present in equal amounts, the body is healthy. When they are out of balance, a person becomes ill.

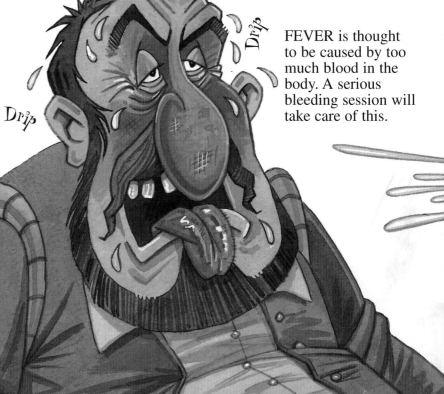

FEVER is thought to be caused by too much blood in the body. A serious bleeding session will take care of this.

A DRY, HACKING COUGH with a fever is caused by too much yellow bile in the body.

Handy Hint
Bad-tempered patients often have too much hot blood. Give them regular blood-lettings to calm them down.

SADNESS AND DEPRESSION are caused by an excess of black bile.

COLDS occur when you have too much phlegm in your body.

13

Battlefield Horrors

One of the worst places to be in the 16th century is in the middle of a war. In 1563, you are officially made a barber surgeon in an army fighting in northern France. Soldiers face guns and muskets as well as swords, arrows, pikes, and axes. The injuries suffered are horrendous, and barber surgeons like you can do very little to help. Conditions are filthy, and there are no antiseptics. Limbs damaged in battle usually become infected and have to be amputated. Several people have to hold the soldier down during surgery. Even though he is given a whack on the head with the surgeon's mallet to knock him out, he will suffer tremendous pain. Few survive long after this dreadful ordeal.

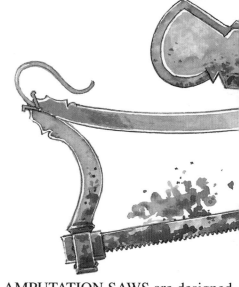

AMPUTATION SAWS are designed to look decorative rather than to amputate limbs properly. Instruments are not washed between operations, and they are often dropped in the mud.

BARBER SURGEONS study battlefield wounds and draw diagrams to show possible injuries (right).

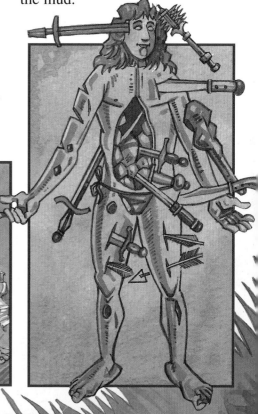

14

Plagued by Infections

Other Nasty Diseases:

ST. VITUS'S DANCE is a disease caused by a bacterial infection. It causes people to jerk and move uncontrollably, as if they are trying to do a wild dance.

LEPROSY is common. This disease eats away at skin and muscle. Because leprosy is easy to spot, lepers are outcasts and are forced to live away from other people.

SCROFULA is a form of tuberculosis. It can be cured, so it is said, by touching royalty. Touching a coin that the monarch has touched is also thought to work.

The Black Death, the largest-ever outbreak of the plague, happened in the mid-1300s. It killed most of the population of Europe and then returned again and again. There is yet another bad outbreak in 1563, and many people leave London. Even Queen Elizabeth I flees to Windsor with her household. To prevent the infection from reaching her, she gives an order that anyone arriving at Windsor from London is to be hung

POP

There is little that you can do for somebody with either the spitting plague or the bubonic plague. Spitting plague makes you cough and spit blood and finishes you off in about three days. Bubonic plague causes huge boil-like lumps called buboes to erupt all over your body. Many die from it in about five days, but if you are still alive after that, you could recover.

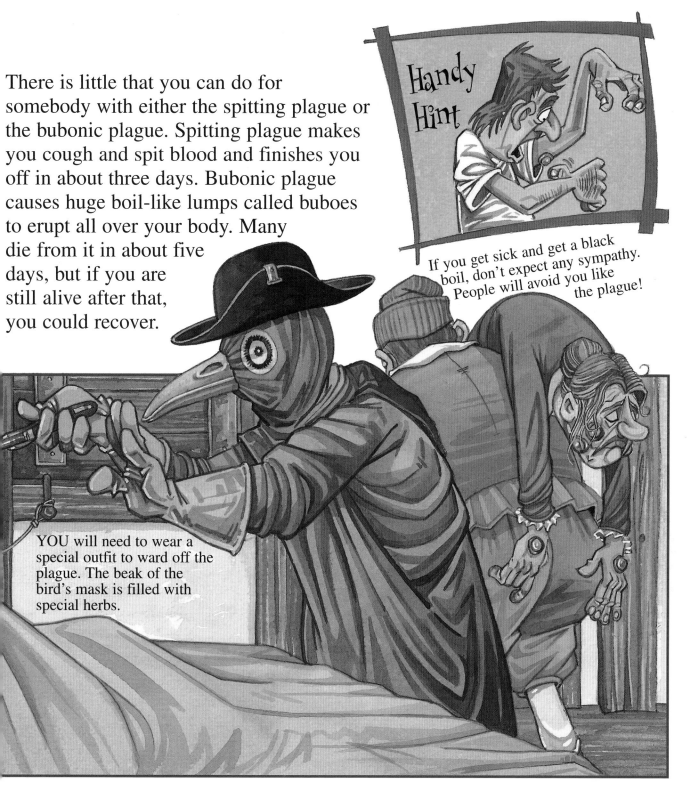

Handy Hint

If you get sick and get a black boil, don't expect any sympathy. People will avoid you like the plague!

YOU will need to wear a special outfit to ward off the plague. The beak of the bird's mask is filled with special herbs.

Hospital Surgery

After your time with the army, you return to England and take a position at St. Bartholomew's hospital in London. Most 16th-century hospitals are places of fear. Although most patients are poor, they are forced to pay the hospital their funeral expenses before they are allowed in. The latest techniques are practiced at St. Bartholomew's: nose jobs, tooth extractions, and cataract operations. Aristocratic soldiers who return from battle with injuries can get false limbs or a false nose made of gold. Some nobles have their noses altered to improve their appearance. This is an early form of plastic surgery.

TREPANNING is carried out by barber surgeons. If you keep getting headaches, you might have a hole drilled into your skull to let the "badness" out.

False Limbs:

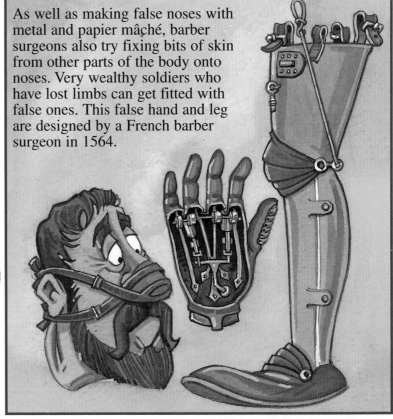

As well as making false noses with metal and papier mâché, barber surgeons also try fixing bits of skin from other parts of the body onto noses. Very wealthy soldiers who have lost limbs can get fitted with false ones. This false hand and leg are designed by a French barber surgeon in 1564.

Oh, would you stay still?
Hope that your patients take some opium or alcohol before operations. This will deaden the pain or even make them sleep through the whole thing!
Handy Hint Z Z Z
This won't hurt... much.

Quacks and Witches

The well-off in Tudor times can afford the services of a physician or a barber surgeon, but most people are too poor. Qualified doctors are also in short supply. This leaves opportunities for quacks, people who sell all sorts of potions and liquors that are supposed to cure everything. Many of them sell their cure-alls at fairs and by the side of the road, and most people are taken in and buy them by the bottle. Barber surgeons hate quacks, but the sad truth is that the barber surgeon's medicines and potions are just as likely to fail. Nobody really has the knowledge to treat many illnesses.

Bottles of potion

Accused of Witchcraft?

Maybe I should have drowned.

Guaranteed to make you live 'til you're ninety!

WOMEN who make herbal remedies from the plants around them are often accused of witchcraft. The test for a witch is to bind the woman in a sack or put her on a ducking stool, and then throw her in a river. If she floats, she is a witch. If she sinks, she is not. Women proved to be witches are burned at the stake.

Herbs and the Apothecary

JOHN GERARD grows his own herbs and writes a famous book on herbalism. Several other herbalists publish books during the 1500s.

pothecaries and herbalists are becoming very important, and you work with several of them. You meet John Gerard, one of the greatest herbalists of the time. He is himself a surgeon, and he has traveled widely. He grows more than a thousand plants to treat his patients. Gerard will publish his own guide to herbal medicine in 1597.

Gerard boils different herbs in oil and extracts their essence. He rubs these highly fragrant oils into the skin of patients. You often ask him to make up herbal treatments. One of them, willow bark, is used as a treatment for pain. Willow bark contains a very potent ingredient that actually does dull pain.

Barbaric Births

What You Might Need:

A BIRTHING CHAIR has a large hole in the seat for the baby to pass through. The long skirts of the mother are draped around the chair for modesty.

FORCEPS can pull a baby out, but in unskilled hands they can cause severe injuries, so be careful!

You might not want to be sick in the 16th century, but it can be even worse to be a woman. Girls marry at very young ages — twelve or thirteen — and then have children constantly. Childbirth is dangerous. Many women die in labor or after birth because of infection. Many babies also die.

AAARGGHH!

Only noblewomen are attended by a barber surgeon. If things go wrong, you could use forceps to pull the baby out. Your knowledge of anatomy also allows you to carry out a cesarean, an operation to remove a baby through its mother's abdomen.

Handy Hint

Tell all your pregnant patients that they should make arrangements for the baby's birth — and for its funeral, just in case.

Perhaps it's time to use the knife.

Congratulations!

MIDWIVES attend women giving birth and take care of them afterwards. They aren't trained, but they learn from other midwives and generally do a good job.

25

At War Again – the Armada

Between 1577 and 1580, you are the barber surgeon on the *Golden Hind*, the ship captained by Sir Francis Drake. Sailors are often sick. They are always wet, and they barely sleep on the boards below deck. Their diet of salt pork, beef, cheese, dried fish, and biscuits gives them scurvy.

In 1588, you are barber surgeon on Drake's ship during the Spanish Armada. On July 21, Drake attacks the Armada near Plymouth. The Armada is beaten, but the cost to sailors is high. Many suffer terrible injuries after being shot or trapped behind cannons.

Splash!

Scurvy

Scurvy is caused by not eating enough vitamin C, but you don't know that. You find that some herbs help, particularly when eaten fresh.

End of an Era

After the success of the Armada, Queen Elizabeth I recognizes your bravery. She makes you one of her personal physicians for the last five years of her life. This is not always a pleasant experience — she becomes bad-tempered and bitter as she gets older. In February 1603, you are called to her. She has been walking in the cold air and has caught a chill. For two weeks you go to her every day, advising rest and giving hot infusions of different herbs.

ARCHBISHOP WHITGIFT, the Archbishop of Canterbury, is the only man whom Queen Elizabeth I wants with her as she is dying. Her doctors are all turned away.

Go away — you can do nothing for me now.

In mid-March, however, the queen decides never to see any of her doctors again. She lies on cushions, hardly eating or drinking. You call for another week but are refused an audience. Elizabeth falls into a deep sleep, and on the morning of March 24, 1603, she dies. The Tudor age has ended.

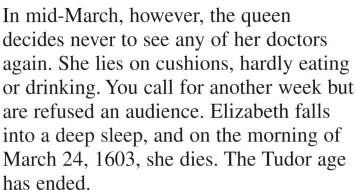

Handy Hint

A new fashion for smoking has just begun. Avoid this at all costs, as it is particularly bad for your health.

YOU TEACH a group of apprentices during the last fifteen years of your career, just as your master did fifty years ago. You die at the age of seventy-two, a grand old age for someone who has spent his life mixing with the sick of the 16th century.

See what it says about an orangey color.

Glossary

Amputation Cutting off someone's limb, usually a leg.

Anatomy The branch of science that deals with the structure of the body, including the bones in the skeleton, how the muscles are attached to them, and what the major organs are like.

Antiseptic A substance that kills germs.

Apprentice Someone who is learning a craft, trade, or profession.

Astrology Predicting the future by looking at the positions of the stars.

Barber surgeon A general doctor who treats the sick by doing minor operations and recommending herbal potions. The name comes from before Tudor times, when this role was taken by a man who also cut hair, trimmed beards, and extracted teeth.

Bile A green, bitter liquid produced by a small gland just below the liver.

Cataract A milky skin that forms on the eyes, particularly in older people. It can cause blindness.

Diagnosis Identification of a patient's illness by looking at the symptoms.

Dissection Cutting up the body to study what is inside.

Ducking stool A low stool attached to a frame. In Tudor times, a form of punishment was to be put on the stool and ducked underneath the water of a lake or pond.

Essence Parts of plants and flowers obtained by boiling them up and concentrating the resulting liquid.

Fever A rise in body temperature. Severe fevers can be very dangerous and even deadly.

Herbalism The treating of illness using mixtures and preparations of herbs.

Infusion A liquid prepared by boiling a plant or herb and given to the patient as a health-giving drink.

Leeches Small, sluglike animals that suck blood.

Mallet A blunt hammer that surgeons used to knock out patients who needed serious surgery, such as a leg amputation.

Midwife A woman who looks after another woman while she gives birth to a baby.

Musket A type of gun.

Opium A drug made from poppies.

Phlegm The gooey substance produced by the lungs and linings of the nose and throat.

Pike A long, spearlike weapon used by 16th-century soldiers.

Plague A disease spread by rats that caused many deaths during the 14th, 15th, and 16th centuries.

Potent Very powerful.

Remedy A treatment.

Trepanning The practice of cutting a hole in a human skull to let out evil spirits.

Urine The liquid produced by the kidneys and lost from the body as waste.

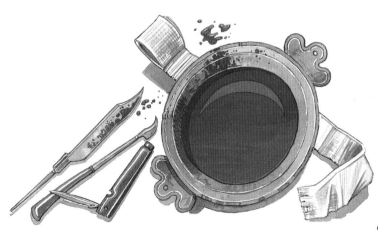

Index